TINY GARDEN, HUGE HARVEST

HOW TO HARVEST HUGE CROPS FROM TINY PLOTS AND CONTAINER GARDENS

Caleb Warnock

THE BACKYARD RENAISSANCE COLLECTION

DISCOVER THE LONG-LOST SKILLS OF SELF-RELIANCE

y name is Caleb Warnock, and I've been working for years to learn how to return to forgotten skills, the skills of our ancestors. As our world becomes increasingly unstable, self-reliance becomes invaluable. Throughout this collection, The Backyard Renaissance, I will share with you the lost skills of self-sufficiency and healthy living. Come with me and other do-it-yourself experimenters and rediscover the joys and successes of simple self-reliance.

FAMILIUS

Published by Familius LLC, www.familius.com

Familius books are available at special discounts for bulk purchases, whether for sales promotions or for family or corporate use. For more information, contact Familius Sales at 559-876-2170 or email orders@familius.com.

Library of Congress Cataloging-in-Publication Data
LCCN: 2016961876

Print ISBN 9781942934844
Ebook ISBN 9781944822415

Printed in the United States of America

Edited by Julie Levitan
Cover design by David Miles
Book design by David Miles and Kurt Wahlner

10 9 8 7 6 5 4 3 2 1

First Edition

TINY GARDEN, HUGE HARVEST

Dedicated in memoriam to my grandparents, Robert and Phyllis Warnock, who had the largest vegetable garden I ever saw and gave me strawberry plants and a pamphlet on how to grow them when I was in elementary school. My lifelong gardening obsession may be entirely your fault!

I miss you.

CONTENTS

WELCOME TO TINY GARDEN, HUGE HARVEST

In this book, you will find:

- Simple, effective techniques to maximize your harvest
- Information to help choose the right crops for your garden—and you
- Tips and tricks to better manage your garden
- Design advice and examples for even the tiniest garden
- A design worksheet and crop index to help create your own tiny garden (and a huge harvest)

THE BENEFITS OF A TINY GARDEN

A garden, small or large, allows us to reap the benefits of self-reliance and also gives us an opportunity to pass those lessons onto our children and grandchildren. Establishing a garden at home allows any family access to delicious, organic food without having to worry about the cost at the grocery store. Unfortunately, many families assume that because they don't have the time and space to maintain a larger garden, they can't have any garden at all.

But that's not true! For busy families, a tiny garden creates a manageable and sustainable workload. And for some people, a tiny garden means they can downsize when an existing large garden becomes impossible for health or time reasons.

I have had gardens of every size. My freshman year at college, my entire garden was in pots in the window. I even grew squash. I was crazy. I wasn't homesick, but I was super-sick of living in a rabbit hutch, crammed in with five roommates (even though they were the best roommates ever). Today, my garden may be the largest in my state. So I feel I can speak with authority on the benefits of both. The benefits of a tiny garden are the same benefits of living in a tiny house—you spend much less time maintaining and cleaning. I have seen so many people become overwhelmed with their large gardens because they are designed wrong (big gardens are only possible when designed very carefully). People with tiny gardens are much less likely to give up on gardening, even when their garden is designed wrong. (For information on how to correctly design a garden, see my *Successful Gardening* class at SeedRenaissance.com.)

In November 2015, I harvested:

- 105 pounds of carrots from a 10-foot-by-2-foot bed
- 40 pounds of beets from a 6-foot-by-2-foot bed
- 34 pounds of parsnips from a 10-foot-by-2-foot bed
- 28 pounds of turnips from a 6-foot-by-2-foot bed

This is a total of 207 pounds of produce. Based on the prices at a local store, these organic vegetables would have cost me $847. Instead, I got all this from 64 square feet of garden—that's just 8 by 8 feet!

Harvesting these huge amounts from such a small space was only possible because of the strategies that I've developed over the years. In the next section, you will find tips and tricks to help you get a huge harvest no matter how tiny your garden space is—whether it is a balcony or a bantam backyard.

HUGE HARVEST TIPS AND TECHNIQUES

SUCCESSION CROPPING

This strategy involves planting and harvesting a series of different vegetables, one after the other. For example, in autumn, you might plant orach—a cousin of spinach—and harvest it throughout the autumn and winter under a cloche or cold frame. Then, in early spring, you would pull out the orach and plant radishes in the same spot. After harvesting the radishes in early summer, you could replace those again with lettuce. Then, in late May, you would pull out the lettuce and replace it with squash. Finally, when the squash is finished in autumn, you could replace it with orach and start the cycle again.

If you are new to gardening, you may think it strange to plan your garden cycle beginning in autumn, when most people are finished gardening. But for gardeners who practice self-reliance, the true garden cycle begins, not ends, in autumn.

You can read more about year-round gardening in my book *Backyard Winter Gardening*.

The chart opposite offers some other succession crop options. Example 1 demonstrates a true succession rotation, in which different vegetables are planted each harvest. Example 2 offers a simpler rotation involving just two vegetables.

In Example 3, you will notice that I suggest you plant peas to harvest for pea greens in early spring and that those same pea plants remain in the garden so that you can harvest the actual pea pods in late spring. This is an example of getting two harvests from a single vegetable. You can see a different example of this concept in Example 4, where I suggest you plant turnips in early spring for harvesting the turnip greens; those same turnips are left in the garden so you can harvest the root bulbs in late spring. The next section offers more details on this method.

Succession Cropping

	Autumn (plant in July-Aug)	Winter (plant in Aug-Sept in cold frame)	Early Spring (plant in Feb-Mar in cold frame)	Late Spring (plant in Mar-Apr)	Early Summer (plant in Apr-May)
Ex. 1	Carrots	Komatsuna	Orach	Radishes	Cucumbers
Ex. 2	Swiss Chard	Swiss Chard (stays)	Carrots	Carrots (stay)	Carrots (stay)
Ex. 3	Beets	Fettle	Peas Greens	Peas (stay)	Broccoli
Ex. 4	Spinach	Collard Greens	Turnips	Turnips (stay)	Basil

GREENS-TO-ROOTS HARVESTING

Unlike true succession cropping, with this method you start by harvesting greens over a long time and end by harvesting the root vegetable. For example, you can plant a Chioggia beet in late spring or early autumn. It grows quickly, and within three weeks, you can harvest the outer leaves, which are wonderful raw in salads or cooked on their own. You do not take the center leaves, which will always be baby leaves because beets produce leaves from the center outward. Since beets produce leaves from the center outwards, you should only harvest the outermost leaves. Cutting down the inner leaves too much may prevent the beetroot from growing properly. You can harvest the outer leaves of each plant about every ten days through autumn, winter, spring, and early summer. That's a huge harvest from one tiny plant. Then, just when the weather begins to warm, you harvest the bulb for eating.

Many other root vegetables—and even peas—are great options for greens-to-roots harvesting. These varieties include:

- **Beets:** Albino sugar beets, Chioggia beets, Early Wonder beets
- **Peas:** Cascadia peas, Sugar Ann peas, Golden Sweet peas

- **Turnips:** When harvesting turnip leaves, take the outer leaves when they are very young. The older leaves get an unpleasant prickly texture. The prickly leaves should be left alone to help the plant begin producing a bulb.
- **Rutabaga:** The leaves are edible, but make sure to take only outer leaves.
- **Celariac and parsley root:** Harvest biggest leaves.

Special note: Any immature squash can be eaten, so you can take some immature (small) pumpkins and use them like summer squash as well as all late-developing baby squashes that will never have time to grow to full size because they were "born" too late in summer.

TIP: BOLTING

WHEN ANY OF THE PLANTS BEGIN TO PRODUCE A SEED STALK–CALLED "BOLTING"–REMOVE THE BOLTED STALK AS SOON AS POSSIBLE. WITHIN A FEW DAYS, THE PLANT WILL TRY TO BOLT AGAIN AND MAY TRY TO BOLT SEVERAL SIDE STEMS AT A TIME. REMOVE ALL BOLTED STALKS AS SOON AS POSSIBLE AND CONTINUE TO RE-MOVE THEM TO EXTEND THE HARVEST. YOUNG, TENDER BOLTS CAN BE EATEN. EVENTUALLY, THOUGH, THE PLANT WILL NATURALLY DIE.

GREENS HARVESTING

Like the "greens" portion of greens-to-roots harvesting, this technique involves repeatedly harvesting the leaves of one plant every few weeks. This way, you can harvest huge amounts of produce from a single plant all year round!

For example, you can plant Caleb's Deep Winter lettuce—a variety I developed myself—in late spring or early autumn. It grows quickly and will be ready to harvest within about a month. Instead of harvesting the whole plant, harvest only the largest leaves. The smaller leaves, which are found in the center of the plant, continue to grow out. In roughly ten days, those smaller center leaves will have become the larger outer leaves. Again, pick just those larger leaves, and thus the cycle continues! With this method, you can harvest the same plant about every ten days through autumn, winter, spring, and early summer.

This kind of harvesting has been the key to self-sufficient eating for my family and me. Instead of relying solely on lettuce for salads, we use a colorful, flavorful mix of greens. I've found that a tightly planted mix of Deep Winter lettuce, Winter Green Jewel romaine, Mizuna salad greens, Komatsuna salad greens, Vernal Red orach, and America spinach can produce roughly a gallon bag of salad greens per week in only 2 square feet of garden space. That can include almost every week of the year if you protect your garden with shade in the summer and cold frames or cloches in the winter.

This may sound like a lot of plants for such a small space, but I've found that overplanting is the best strategy when it comes to greens. The overcrowding encourages lettuces and salad greens to grow upright instead of sprawling out, which keeps the leaves clean and produces more pounds of produce per square foot.

Tightly planted lettuce in the author's greenhouse.

Other varieties for greens harvesting include:

- **Lettuces:** All varieties at SeedRenaissance.com
- **America spinach**
- **Komatsuna salad greens**
- **Mizuna salad greens**
- **Osaka Purple mustard greens**
- **Pac Choi, Tai Sai, Wong Bok**
- **Orach**
- **Caleb's Winter Fine Fettle greens**
- **Celery and Par-Cel**
- **Swiss chard**
- **Michihili Chinese cabbage:** Treat this as a loose-leaf lettuce, taking only the largest leaves. It will never develop a solid, large head when treated like this, but it will give you a huge, long harvest!
- **Vates collard greens**
- **Broccoli:** When harvesting broccoli, take the main head quickly when it's at a small size. This encourages side sprouts of broccoli to begin forming immediately, which extends the broccoli harvest over months. Broccoli greens are also edible. The greens taste best when young, but don't take too many or you may kill the plant.

- **Kale:** Take only the outer leaves. If the kale begins to bolt, remove the bolt repeatedly to extend the harvest. The bolt and flowers are also edible.

TIP: CUT, DON'T PINCH

WHEN HARVESTING GREENS, CUT THE LEAVES OFF WITH A KNIFE OR CLIPPERS. PINCHING THE LEAVES BY HAND OFTEN PULLS AT THE ROOT OF THE PLANT AND DAMAGES THE HAIR-ROOTS. THIS EITHER SLOWS THE GROWTH OF THE PLANT OR KILLS IT, ESPECIALLY AFTER MULTIPLE HARVESTS. I USE A KITCHEN STEAK KNIFE TO SLICE THE LEAVES CLEANLY OFF THE MAIN STEM. GARDEN SHEARS AND CLIPPERS WORK WELL TOO, BUT I'VE FOUND THAT STEAK KNIVES ARE BEST FOR MAKING PRECISE, CLEAN CUTS.

FOUR-SEASON GARDENING

You'll notice that each of these techniques includes a winter harvest. If you have a tiny garden, one of the easiest ways to maximize your harvest is to grow food 365 days a year. In order to do this, you will need to invest in cloches, cold frames, or

The author's geothermal winter greenhouse.

a greenhouse to protect your garden from the cold. You can find more information in my book *Backyard Winter Gardening* and a full list of the best vegetables for planting in autumn and winter at SeedRenaissance.com.

FREEZE AND MOVE ON

When a plant is ready to harvest, we are not necessarily ready to eat it. In this situation, harvest the whole crop anyway, then blanch and freeze it. This frees up space to immediately plant the next succession crop.

Blanching is a process that partially cooks vegetables so

that they can better retain their color and nutritional value when frozen. First, you will wash, trim, and chop the vegetables into whatever shape you prefer. Then you will boil them for 90 seconds. The blanched vegetables are then spread into a single layer over a cookie sheet and frozen solid overnight. Once they are frozen, you can put them all into a single freezer bag and take out whatever amount you want, as needed. Make sure not to skip the step of freezing the vegetables in a single layer. If you put all the vegetables in a bag immediately, they will freeze into one giant lump. You will have to thaw the whole bag at once in order to remove what you want, and frozen vegetables should be thawed only once. Repeated thawing and refreezing damages the flavor, texture, and nutrition of the vegetables.

KNOW WHAT TO GROW

Choosing the right crops for your garden depends on quite a few factors, including the size, shape, and orientation of the garden and your personal taste, of course. There are also certain varieties that simply yield a bigger harvest. The following sections are full of advice and information to help you choose the best crops for you.

GROW WHAT YOU EAT MOST

This may seem obvious at first, but surprisingly, many people fail to take this into consideration. Take the time to really think about what your family will use the most. There is no point in using space for food that will only go to waste.

For example, if your family is having green smoothies every morning (a simple and delicious way to get your daily dose of greens), you are likely spending a lot of money buying greens that you could easily be growing. If you are making smoothies that often, you may want to devote the majority of your garden to growing greens.

On the other hand, if you are a "meat and potatoes" kind of person, you may want to devote most of your garden to root vegetables. If you are gardening simply for the enjoyment of a summer harvest of fresh food, you may want to give over most of your space to tomatoes, corn, and watermelon. Consider your goals carefully, and map out all the garden space you have to match these goals.

GAME SHOW GARDENING

Let's play a game! What produces the most in the least space? The winner gets a larger harvest! When you understand that some vegetables simply produce more in a small space than others, it begins to change the way you think about garden strategies and designs.

ROUND 1: CARROTS VS. POTATOES

Carrots win, by a long shot. You can get more harvest by weight from carrots per square foot than from potatoes. Why? Because many carrot plants can fit into the space required for one potato plant.

ROUND 2: CORN VS. ANY OTHER VEGETABLE

Corn always loses. One corn plant takes up a lot of space for a small harvest of only one or two ears. Corn also shades the other garden plants around it, meaning those plants will produce a smaller harvest because they are getting fewer hours of direct sunlight.

LETTUCE VS. A MIX OF LETTUCES AND SALAD GREENS

The mix wins! While lettuce is the traditional salad ingredient, many people have now discovered that a salad of mixed greens is not only tastier but also more nutritious. In the space that one butterhead lettuce might grow, you can grow ten plants of Mizuna salad greens, and you will get five to ten times the harvest. The same goes for Komatsuna, fettle greens, collard greens, orach, spinach, and more. And speaking of Komatsuna . . .

KOMATSUNA VS. ANY OTHER SALAD GREEN

Komatsuna wins! Most gardeners have never heard of this wonderful Japanese salad green, but after discovering it when I lived in Japan, I have been growing it for years. This is a green that anyone who loves salad should be growing. More than 3,500 people have toured my garden in the past three years; the result is that many people now tell me that they are beginning to grow Komatsuna after tasting it in my garden. The best thing about Komatsuna, however, is that this champion of the salad world can grow four times more greens per square inch than any other green I have ever grown!

FRUIT TREE VS. GARDEN

Garden wins. Based on square footage, you can get more pounds of produce from a garden than you can from a fruit tree. One fruit tree may produce 50 pounds of peaches, but the space that tree takes up could give you $850 of produce in a summer garden. Ideally, you could grow both fruit trees and vegetables, but in a tiny garden, you may have space for only one or the other.

One of the author's backyard vegetable gardens.

That being said, if you do have the space for fruit trees, I recommend growing raspberries. Many people are hesitant to plant raspberries, since they are known to spread slowly over time. In my experience, though, there are always people who are happy to have any extra raspberry plants from my garden. I give mine away for free, but I know other gardeners who sell them inexpensively.

EARLY DAY-COUNT VARIETIES

Some vegetable varieties, also known as "cultivars," are ready to harvest earlier than others. This is perhaps the least understood part of gardening and the misconception that most frustrates unwitting gardeners. If you're looking to make the most of your harvest, grow only varieties that are early to harvest. These vegetables are known as "early day-count varieties," meaning they have the least number of days to maturity. Seed Renaissance.com offers only early day-count varieties. Here are two examples to demonstrate the concept of day count.

TOMATOES

Say you want to grow some good slicing tomatoes and you're deciding between the "Joe's Earliest Slicer" and the "German

TIP: KEEPING COUNT

IT'S IMPORTANT TO BE AWARE THAT THESE DAY COUNTS ARE LONGER THAN THE TIME A PLANT SPENDS IN THE GARDEN. FOR SEEDS, THE DAY COUNT STARTS WHEN THE PLANT'S SECOND SET OF LEAVES, CALLED "TRUE LEAVES," REACH FULL SIZE. FOR A TRANSPLANT, THE COUNT BEGINS AFTER IT HAS BEEN REPLANTED, WHEN THE FIRST NEW SET OF LEAVES REACH FULL SIZE. BOTH SEEDS AND TRANSPLANTS WILL BE IN THE GARDEN FOR THREE-TO FOUR WEEKS BEFORE THEIR DAY COUNT BEGINS.

THIS CAN BE A PROBLEM IF, LIKE ME, YOU HAVE AN AVERAGE TWENTY-NINE-DAY GROWING SEASON. SAY YOU PLANT BRANDYWINE TOMATOES, WHICH HAVE A NINTEY-DAY COUNT. EVEN THOUGH THE DAY COUNT IS TECHNICALLY LOWER THAN THE DAYS IN THE SEASON, YOU'RE NOT LIKELY TO HARVEST MANY OF THESE TOMATOES. WHEN YOU ADD THE THREE TO FOUR WEEKS (APPROXIMATELY THIRTY DAYS) BEFORE THE DAY COUNT BEGINS, YOU WILL FIND THAT BRANDYWINE TOMATOES NEED ABOUT 120 DAYS TO HARVEST.

Queen." Both produce great fruit, but the Joe's Earliest Slicer matures in only forty to forty-five days, while the German Queen takes nearly one hundred. This means that by simply choosing the right variety, you can get nearly two times the harvest!·

PEAS

Consider the "Tom's Thumb" peas—a fifty day-count variety—and the "Lincoln" peas—an eighty-five day-count variety.

If you were to plant both "Tom Thumb" and "Lincoln" peas in your garden on the same day, you would start eating fresh Tom Thumb peas at least a month before you would see any ripe Lincoln peas.

PERENNIALS AND SELF-SEEDING VARIETIES

Perennial vegetables are especially easy and useful—they just live in your garden year after year, gifting you with a harvest. At least a few self-seeding vegetables must be allowed to go to seed if you want a harvest year after year. In a tiny garden, you need to think carefully about how much space you want to devote to any particular self-seeding vegetable. It will likely be necessary to remove extra plants that you don't want. For example, if you allow the Dwarf Blue Siberian kale to self-seed, you may get many kale plants, so you will need to remove some of the baby plants. However, removing some self-seeded plants is always easier than planting from seed because self-seeded plants work with Mother Nature, germinating at the correct time and needing very little (if any) attention from you, the gardener.

WILD EDIBLES

You find many free salad greens, and even some root vegetables, in public spaces and in the "weeds" from your garden. These include blue mustard, mallow, wild spinach, and dandelions. In my house, we eat many wild edibles. Recently, while weeding in my garden, I ate all the purslane that I pulled out right there on the spot!

When harvesting wild edibles, there is just one rule of thumb: get them from a clean space. I have had more than 3,000 people tour my garden, and many of them have remarked that my pasture is a virtual forest of wild edibles. I

Greens and edible flowers from the author's garden.

always point out to them that harvesting food that has been walked on by the dog, the horse, or the cows is not a great idea. We eat wild edibles only from my garden space, because I know they are clean—even I don't walk on them.

GARDENING IN THE SHADE

Many gardeners have unrealized potential garden space under a tree, on the north side of their house, or even in a windowsill that doesn't get direct sunlight. Some people have come to my classes because they have only shady areas to garden in because they own or rent a home without a sunny garden spot. They are thrilled to learn that they have a huge range of options despite their shady conditions.

When growing in dappled or full shade, expect slower growth and smaller sized leaves and bulbs. But if you have a tiny garden, finding shady areas to expand is a key step to successful self-reliant eating.

Strawberries, arugula, radishes, and kale are just a few of the many vegetables that grow well in partial or even complete shade. For a full list of shady gardening options, see the Crop Index beginning on page 53.

Designing Your Garden

All of the techniques I've listed work toward helping you expand your harvest, even without expanding your space. But even a tiny garden can be "expanded" with the right strategies and designs.

You can put some potted herbs in a kitchen window. Remove a tree. Borrow a garden. Convert your lawn to a garden. Convert the parking strip to a garden—though you should check first to make sure that is allowed by your city. I even know several people who garden on their roofs. My beloved cousin even kept her bees on the roof of her carport. You can line your sidewalk with growing containers. Use your porch and balcony as much as possible. You can hang pots from the house.

The most important thing is to consider your space and your goals before setting up your garden. The following sections are full of design advice and examples to help you make the most of your tiny garden.

Two examples of balcony gardens near downtown Boston.

DETERMINE YOUR GOALS: SELF-RELIANCE VS. ENJOYMENT

Before you begin designing your garden, it's important to determine whether your goal is self-reliance or simply enjoyment. Let me first be clear that both kinds of gardens are enjoyable. But self-reliant gardens should be designed to put hearty food on the table, while enjoyment gardens can be designed with only the pleasure of gardening in mind.

A self-reliant garden will need to contain a variety of vegetables that can provide real sustenance. The example below is

Self-reliant garden layout.

Carrots					Onions	
Beets		Greens	Parsnips		Tomato	
Golden Turnips					Squash	

a self-reliant garden that has been designed to focus on root vegetables, which are a keystone to putting real, hearty food on the table. This garden also includes space for greens, which are an important nutritional component. Finally, two smaller spaces are left for tomatoes, which are easy to freeze, and squash.

Of course, this is not the only possible design. A self-reliant garden can—and should—be tailored to your needs. Consider your garden space and your personal vegetable preferences before deciding what to plant and how much.

That sentiment applies even more for enjoyment gardens. If you're gardening purely for pleasure, than you should plant

Enjoyment garden layout.

Corn				
Tomatoes	Tomatoes	Beans		Melons
Peppers	Lettuce	Spinach		Melons
Flowers	Mixed Salad Greens			Melons

any fruit or vegetable that you want, even if they aren't likely to produce a huge harvest. For example, the garden below devotes sections to corn and flowers. While I wouldn't recommend either of these for a self-reliant garden, they are perfectly fine in this case. This enjoyment garden is designed to provide all the old-fashioned pleasures you remember from eating fresh from Grandma and Grandpa's summer garden.

You'll notice that both examples provide space for small walking paths. It is always important to make sure you have easy access to all parts of the garden for weeding, watering, inspecting for bugs, checking ripeness, and—most importantly—harvesting.

Both of these examples are 6-by-13-foot traditional gardens, meaning that they are planted directly in the soil. These measurements can be adjusted depending on your space and needs.

PORCH AND BALCONY GARDENS

If you don't have the lawn space for a traditional garden, a porch or balcony can be a great place to set up a potted garden. When designing this type of garden, the most important

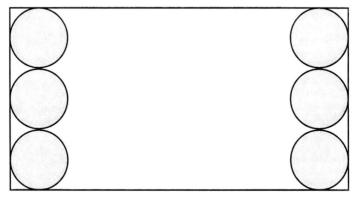

ABOVE: Round balcony garden layout. BELOW: Square balcony garden layout.

thing to consider is surface area. The diagrams above represents two balcony gardens. They are nearly identical—both balconies are the same size and have the same number of pots. The only difference is the shape of those pots.

By simply using square pots instead of round, there is no wasted space and the usable space has nearly doubled. Talk

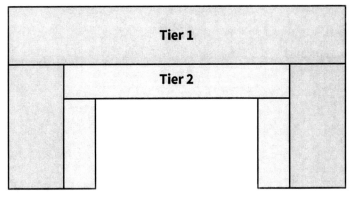

Tiered garden layout.

about maximizing space! This design can even be taken one step further by adding a tier. The diagram below represents a tiered garden using a 2-foot-tall garden box as Tier 1 and a 12-inch-tall garden box as Tier 2. If you create a tiered garden, make sure you fill the second tier with plants that thrive in the shade. The shorter tier usually will be completely shaded, but that won't stop you from collecting a huge harvest.

Now, you might be thinking, *Caleb, your design has taken up a lot of the balcony space!* This is true, but consider two facts. First, in my experience, many balconies become a kind of unsightly storage space that is rarely—if ever—used. Second, a balcony filled with living greenery and flowers will only improve your view from inside. A garden can make your balcony beautiful and useful.

And consider how convenient it is—going to water, maintain, and harvest from your garden literally takes only steps. In the winter, when you want to move some of the herbs and flowers indoors, you will have to move them only a few feet. The more you think about it, the more you will realize that a balcony garden has many benefits.

TIP: COMPOST VS. SOIL

IF YOU ARE GARDENING IN POTS, FILL THEM WITH ORGANIC COMPOST INSTEAD OF NATIVE SOIL. NATIVE SOIL IS FILLED WITH WEEDS. USE ORGANIC COMPOST AND YOUR GARDEN WILL BE TOTALLY WEED-FREE!

HANGING AND VERTICAL GARDENS

HANGING GARDENS

Any suspended pot can create a hanging garden. Pots can be hung from eaves, over balconies, and on porches with any garden hooks. You can create an entire garden up in the air, or you can hang a few pots to supplement an existing garden.

TIP: PAY ATTENTION TO YOUR POTS

IN AREAS WHERE THERE IS HUMIDITY AND RAIN, POTS SHOULD HAVE DRAIN HOLES AT THE BOTTOM. IN ARID PLACES WITHOUT HUMIDITY, THE POTS SHOULD NOT HAVE BOTTOM DRAINAGE HOLES. INSTEAD, DRAINAGE HOLES SHOULD BE ABOUT A THIRD OF THE WAY DOWN FROM THE TOP, BECAUSE IN DRY AREAS, KEEPING POTTED PLANTS ALIVE DEPENDS ON SLOWING EVAPORATION AS MUCH AS POSSIBLE. IN DRY AREAS, HANGING AND POTTED PLANTS THRIVE BETTER IN PARTIAL TO FULL SHADE BECAUSE EVAPORATION IS SLOWED.

NO MATTER WHERE YOU LIVE, KEEP IN MIND THAT LARGER POTS CAN MAKE GARDENING MORE MANAGEABLE. LARGER POTS NEED TO BE WATERED LESS OFTEN BECAUSE THEY RETAIN WATER LONGER. IF YOU'RE BUSY AND CAN'T BABYSIT YOUR PLANTS CONSTANTLY, LARGER POTS MAY HELP YOUR GARDEN SURVIVE.

VERTICAL GARDENS

If you are cramped for space, a vertical garden is a way of creating a large garden in a space the size of a bookshelf. Imagine you are in a library standing in front of a shelf full of books—except instead of books, these shelves are lined with potted plants.

These plants are usually watered with a system in which water is released from a container or barrel at the top of the shelving unit. This water then feeds into the pots on the top shelf. As those pots are saturated, they drain out the bottom (or, in dry areas, out of the side holes) and the drained water is channeled into the pots on the next shelf down. This pattern continues until all of the pots are watered. When the bottom row of shelves is watered, the water at the top can be shut off.

An example of using pallets for creative vertical gardening in a tiny space.

With a little practice, this kind of garden becomes easy to water because you know exactly how long the water needs to be on to reach the bottom shelf. This method is also great for water conservation because very little water is lost out of the system. Even better, as the water drains from one shelf of plants to the next, the water actually becomes a kind of compost tea. You can read more about this in the book I coauthored with Logan Lyons titled *All-Natural Aquaponic Lawns, Gardens & Vertical Gardens*.

In the art of vertical gardening, there are two kinds of plants—those which grow upright and those which hang downward. For example, if you plant lettuce on the top shelf, it will grow upward. But if you plant a tomato there, it will hang downward as it grows, especially if you don't use a tomato cage for support. The diagram on the next page represents a vertical garden with seven shelves labeled A–F.

Shelf A: You'll notice that Shelf A is actually the top of the bookcase. This shelf is reserved for the tallest plants. Options for Shelf A include broccoli, cabbage, cauliflower, celery, collard greens, kale, leeks, parsnips, potatoes, stevia, and raspberries.

Shelves B & E: These shelves are reserved for hanging plants because they allow enough room for the plants to hang down. Hanging options include cantaloupe, cucumbers, pole beans, pumpkins, strawberries, zucchini, and squash.

Shelf A

Tallest plants

Shelf B
Hanging plants
Shelf C
Short, upright, shade tolerant plants
Shelf D
Short, upright, shade tolerant plants
Shelf E
Hanging plants
Shelf F
Short, upright, shade tolerant plants
Shelf G
Short, upright, shade tolerant plants

Vertical garden layout.

Shelves C, D, F & G: These shelves should be used for short upright plants. Keep in mind that these shelves are going to be shaded by the hanging plants, especially in the summer. Consider putting shade-tolerant plants on these shelves. Good options for these shelves include beets, bush beans, carrots, eggplant, chives, herbs, lettuce, onions, peas, peppers, radishes, spinach, swiss chard, and turnips.

TIP: SECURITY IS KEY

MAKE SURE THAT ALL OF YOUR POTS ARE SECURED TO THE SHELVES SO THAT THEY DON'T FALL OUT, ESPECIALLY AS THEY GET HEAVIER. THIS IS USUALLY DONE BY PUTTING A BOARD ACROSS THE SHELF JUST BELOW THE TOP OF THE POTS.

NO GARDEN SPACE AT ALL?

If you *still* don't think you have space for a garden, don't worry! Your dream garden is still possible with a little help from your neighbors and community.

A small community garden in Boston.

BORROW A GARDEN, CREATE A FRIEND

At one point in college, I lived in a place where a garden was not possible. So I promptly went to the next-door neighbors, who were elderly. It was obvious they had once had a garden in their backyard but had abandoned it years before. I introduced myself and said that if they would let me use their water and garden space, they could share the harvest with me. They said yes, and I will be forever grateful to them. I took my college graduation photo in this borrowed garden—I was equally proud of my garden and my degree!

I believe that everyone in need of garden space should seriously consider this option. Not only does it provide fresh food for two families, but you will discover that you can make wonderful new friends, too. Being good neighbors is one of the keys to a successful society, and when you befriend gardeners, you may be surprised by the bonds that form. I have taught this concept for years, and I have now seen my own advice bear fruit (literally!) in the lives of other gardeners. I recently received a message from someone who had taken my advice and borrowed a garden from an elderly neighbor. The friendship that bloomed between these two families had changed the lives of everyone involved.

PUBLIC & PRIVATE FOOD FORESTS

Public permaculture food forests have become increasingly popular. A food forest is a kind of wild garden planted with vegetables that will thrive on their own with little or no human intervention. Thanks to the work of garden and nutrition advocates, more and more people in cities have access to public food forests, where anyone is welcome to harvest. Once again, just make sure that what you are harvesting is clean and hasn't been walked on.

A couple in their community garden plot next to Fenway Park in Boston. An excellent example of doing a lot in a small space.

This spring, I was hired to design and plant three perma-culture food forests. Even private gardeners have begun to install these because they are virtually maintenance-free vege-table gardens. In the food forests that I was hired to design and install, I planted Egyptian Walking onions, perennial shallots, garlic, garlic chives, common chives, peppermint, spearmint, sunchokes, self-seeding lettuce, marjoram, peas, asparagus, lemon balm, and more. For information on food forests, or to purchase a kit for planting your own food forest, visit:

SeedRenaissance.com.

CREATING YOUR OWN TINY GARDEN

ow it's time to put all of the techniques, tips, and designs you have learned to good use. In this section, you will find a worksheet exercise and extensive crop index to help you make key decisions about your own tiny garden.

GARDEN WORKSHEET

1. Where is your garden located? Circle one:

Balcony   Porch   Roof   Vertical/Hanging   Yard

2. How large is your garden? To find this measurement, multiply the length by the width of the garden space.

3. Is your garden in direct sunlight? Draw a picture and label areas of the garden that are in full shade, part shade, or dappled light.

4. Do you own or rent your property? There are some things you may not want to invest in if you are renting.

5. Are you gardening primarily for enjoyment or self-reliance?

6. Favorites: If there are certain produce items you *love*, find space for them! After looking through the crop index for inspiration, list your top six here:

A	
B	
C	
D	
E	
F	

7. Garden map: Create a rough sketch—or use the one from number 3 above. Then choose your crops and map out where you want to plant each one. Make sure you have a plan before you start planting!

An example of a huge harvest from a tiny garden at the Fenway Victory Gardens, established in a public park in Boston during rationing in World War II.

CROP INDEX

This list includes only fruit and vegetable varieties for gardeners looking to get a huge harvest from a limited space. For those who are gardening purely for enjoyment, you may find that some of the produce you would like to grow is missing from this list—corn, for example. For a more extensive selection of seeds, visit SeedRenaissance.com.

* = Crops that grow well in the shade

ASIAN GREENS

Tai Sai

Pac Choi

Wong Bok

BEANS

Purple Podded Pole

Cherry Pole

Early Riser

BEETS*

Albino Sugar beets: These are sweet and delicious but taste nothing like traditional beets.

Chioggia beets: Beautiful cooked or raw because of their red and white circles. They are much sweeter than regular beets because they are part sugar beet.

Early Wonder beets: These traditional beets are the earliest to harvest.

BROCCOLI*

Di Cicco: This variety has an early day count, produces prolific side-sprouts, and is relatively small compared to the harvest it yields.

Any variety: All of the varieties offered at SeedRenaissance.com have early day counts.

CANTALOUPE

Noir des Carmes: This variety is very early, is very prolific, and produces more cantaloupes in a smaller space than any other cantaloupe. Best yet, you never have to guess when they are ripe, because they turn from dark green to orange overnight when they are ready to eat!

CARROTS*

Caleb's Carrot Color Mix: Beautiful and delicious!

Scarlet Nantes: These are the earliest-maturing orange carrots.

Danvers: These orange carrots also have an early day count.

Paris Market: These ball-shaped carrots also have an early day count. They grow well in all soil and are perfect for cold frames.

CELERY*

Par-Cel: This is a kind of celery that is easier to grow, takes less water, and has more flavor than common celery.

CHINESE CABBAGE*

Michihili: This variety is very early to harvest, is hugely prolific, and produces more harvest by weight than any other early Asian green.

CUCUMBER

Marketmore: These green cucumbers are very early to harvest and very prolific. I recommend them for pickling!

Poona Kheera: Even though these cucumbers are yellow, they don't go bitter and can sit for a long time in the garden and still taste great.

EGGPLANT

Little Finger: These lavender-colored eggplants have a great flavor and an early day count. They are even more prolific over a long period of time if you keep them harvested.

FETTLE GREENS

Caleb's Winter Fine Fettle Greens: These greens are early to harvest, can be grown all year, and even produce edible flowers.

FLOWERS

Any space you give to flowers is a space you could be growing vegetables. However, no matter how small my garden has

been, I've always made room for flowers. Flowers are not only beautiful, but they can be useful, too. Some flowers are grown to protect the garden from pests (marigolds and pyrethrum, for example) some are edible, and some can be grown as medicinal herbs. So I leave this decision up to you.

GARLIC CHIVES & COMMON CHIVES

One plant produces enough for you to dry and use for a whole year, but choose these only if you use chives.

HERBS

Summer savory: I use this herb more than any other, and one plant can produce a huge volume.

Oregano: One plant can produce all you ever need, but be careful: oregano spreads like crazy.

Basil: Having fresh basil in your garden is a wonderful thing, but be aware that you probably won't have the space to grow as much as you use.

Thyme: One thyme plant will produce a year's worth of herbs.

Rosemary: Rosemary is tall and skinny, so it doesn't take up much room, and it produces a lot.

Peppermint; spearmint; all mints: Warning: mint tends to spread, too. But if you like mint, it's still a great choice for any garden.

Medicinal herbs: I strongly believe every family should practice herbal medicine to control acute (not chronic) illness. So if you know what you are doing, you should give some space to critical medicinal herbs, depending on what herbs your family needs most.

KALE*

Dwarf Blue Siberian kale: This beautiful blue kale is very early to harvest, yields two harvests a year in spring and fall, and is self-seeding.

Any heirloom kale variety

KOMATSUNA

Komatsuna Asian salad greens: Very prolific and fast growing, we call this green a "cut-and-come-again" variety because it grows back over and over again after being cut.

LETTUCE

Buttercrunch: This bestseller has green leaves and a very early day count, you can harvest the outer leaves or let it form a small head, and it's also a cut-and-come-again variety.

Caleb's Deep Winter: This crispy romaine-type variety is early, green, and lasts longer than all other lettuces without bolting in summer. You can harvest the outer leaves or let it form a head, and it's also a cut-and-come-again variety.

Marvel of Four Seasons: This beautiful mix of bronze, green, purple, and red leaves is early to harvest and full of great flavor. The loose outer leaves can be picked for a continual harvest.

Gabriella: This dark red lettuce looks great in salad and has great flavor, and the loose outer leaves can be picked for a continual harvest.

MIZUNA

Mizuna Asian salad greens: These greens are very prolific, are very fast growing, and are also a cut-and-come-again variety.

ONION

Green Mountain Huge Multiplier: This is the largest onion I've been able to find, producing 4-5-inch onions that come in yellow, green, white, red, and purple. They also grow well in most climates.

Yellow Spanish Sweet Globe: The name says it all, except that they also have an early day count!

ORACH

Vernal Red orach: Don't skip this entry in my list just because you have never heard of orach. Everyone should grow orach. It's a purple green that is very easy to grow, is very early to harvest, and grows all year. It has great nutritional content and can either be used like spinach or left to produce a prolific amount of seeds that are 40 percent protein. It can be eaten boiled or used to make a rye-type flour.

PARSNIPS*

All-American: These are easier to grow than carrots, with an early day count, large roots, and good flavor. Remember that greens are great but roots are sustenance. The key to getting a great parsnip crop is to sow the seeds very early, as soon as the ground can be worked in February or March, because Mother Nature will sprout them for you without you needing to water them. They can be sowed in April or May, but you will have to keep the seeds moist for a couple weeks until they germinate.
Hollow Crown: Also easier to grow than carrots, with an early day count, large roots, and good flavor.

PEAS*

Jump: These produce four times more peas than any other pea variety.
Cascadia: These are great for spring, autumn, winter, and greenhouse harvesting. They are prolific and early to harvest.

PEPPERS

Jimmy Nardello: These long, sweet, red peppers are very prolific and among the earliest to harvest of all peppers.

California Wonder: These are also among the earliest to harvest of all peppers. They are sweet green bell peppers that turn red if left on the plant.

Etiuda: These sweet orange bell peppers are among the earliest of all peppers.

PUMPKINS

Potimarron: These pumpkins have thick flesh and a delicious, sweet taste and can provide a full family meal. They are early to harvest and very prolific.

Atlantic Giant: These aren't as great as the Potimarron, but they are a good second option.

RADISHES*

Cincinnati Market: Since these are a carrot-type radish—meaning they are the size and shape of carrots—you get a far greater harvest by weight. They also taste great and grow quickly.

RASPBERRIES

Everbearing: This may be controversial, but I tell everyone that if you grow nothing else, grow raspberries. Every child loves to pick fresh raspberries, and we need to do whatever we can to get children to love the garden and spend time there. White raspberries (also called "champagne raspberries") are sweeter and earlier to harvest than red raspberries. Also, one raspberry plant will produce a far larger harvest by weight than one strawberry plant. To get the largest harvest, choose an everbearing raspberry variety, not a June-bearing variety.

SPINACH*

America: These are very early to harvest and have a long harvest period when you take only the outside leaves.

STEVIA*

Though this herb requires shade and low humidity to grow, it produces very sweet leaves that you can use in place of sugar. See my book *The Stevia Solution* for more information.

SWISS CHARD*

TOMATOES

Joe's Earliest Slicer: This red slicing tomato is the earliest out of 650 varieties I've tried in my garden, and it produces tomatoes all season.

Stupice: This red tomato is also extremely early to harvest and is great for sandwiches and sauces.

Winter Grape: This variety produces more tomatoes, by pound, than any other variety of the 650 I have grown in my garden. The tomatoes are pear-shaped and about the size of a golf ball.

TURNIPS*

Des Vertus Mareau: These white salad turnips are sweeter than all other turnips and are even great raw. They are early to harvest and are good for spring, autumn, and greenhouse harvesting.

Golden: These yellow turnips have a better, less bitter flavor than purple turnips and are early to harvest.

ZUCCHINI

Early Prolific Straight-Neck Summer Squash: This variety is earliest to harvest with an edible skin and a great flavor.

Dark Green Zucchini: These green zukes are early to harvest, prolific, and have a good flavor.

Black Beauty Zucchini: These, too, are early to harvest, prolific, and have a great flavor.

ABOUT THE AUTHOR

Caleb Warnock lives on the bench of the Rocky Mountains with his wife and family. He is the popular author of fourteen books, including *Forgotten Skills of Self-Sufficiency Used by the Mormon Pioneers, The Art of Baking with Natural Yeast, Backyard Winter Gardening, More Forgotten Skills*, and the Backyard Renaissance Collection. When he's not gardening and writing, he enjoys drawing, painting, teaching, and creating new recipes. He sells pure, non-GMO, non-hybrid seeds at SeedRenaissance.com, where you can sign up for his newsletter. Find his YouTube channel at:

https://www.youtube.com/channel/
UCbtYTB1zTUafWU3tHJ_8Hvg.

ABOUT FAMILIUS

VISIT OUR WEBSITE: www.familius.com

JOIN OUR FAMILY: There are lots of ways to connect with us! Subscribe to our newsletters at www.familius.com to receive uplifting daily inspiration, essays from our Pater Familius, a free ebook every month, and the first word on special discounts and Familius news.

GET BULK DISCOUNTS: If you feel a few friends and family might benefit from what you've read, let us know and we'll be happy to provide you with quantity discounts. Simply email us at orders@familius.com.

CONNECT:

www.facebook.com/paterfamilius
@familiustalk, @paterfamilius1
www.pinterest.com/familius

FAMILIUS

THE MOST IMPORTANT WORK YOU EVER DO WILL BE WITHIN THE WALLS OF YOUR OWN HOME.

CPSIA information can be obtained
at www.ICGtesting.com
Printed in the USA
LVOW10s2123221216
518169LV00001B/2/P